# TRAVELER. HONG I

## Navigating the Metropolis, Insider Tips for Getting Around Hong Kong with Ease

### Harris Marvin

# TABLE OF CONTENT

INTRODUCTION

CHAPTER ONE

History Culture and Geography of Hong Kong

CHAPTER TWO

Planning Your Trip

CHAPTER THREE

Major cities in Hong Kong and Transportation options

CHAPTER FOUR

Accommodations (Hotels, Resorts, and Camping Sites)

CHAPTER FIVE

Ancient Monuments, Museums, and Shopping Malls alls in Hong Kong

CHAPTER SIX

Local Cuisines, Drinks, and Street Food in Hong Kong

CHAPTER SEVEN

Vaccines and Emergency Management

CHAPTER EIGHT

Basic Greetings in Hong Kong

CONCLUSION

# INTRODUCTION

Welcome to the vibrant and bustling city of Hong Kong! Nestled on the southeastern coast of China, Hong Kong is a captivating destination that seamlessly blends East and West, tradition and modernity, and natural beauty with towering skyscrapers. As one of the world's most dynamic and cosmopolitan cities, Hong Kong offers an array of experiences that will leave you mesmerized.

With its rich history, diverse culture, and stunning landscapes, Hong Kong has something to offer every traveler. Whether you are an adventurer seeking thrilling experiences, a food lover eager to sample a wide range of delicious cuisines, a shopaholic in search of the latest fashion trends, or a culture enthusiast looking to immerse yourself in ancient traditions, Hong Kong has it all.

This travel guide will serve as your comprehensive companion to exploring the city's many facets. From iconic landmarks such as Victoria Peak and the Big Buddha to hidden gems like local street markets and traditional fishing villages, we will take you on a journey through the vibrant neighborhoods and breathtaking landscapes that define Hong Kong.

Get ready to be captivated by the mesmerizing skyline as you stroll along the bustling streets of Central and experience the energy of the city's financial heart. Indulge in a culinary adventure, from mouthwatering dim sum to tantalizing street food delicacies. Discover the ancient traditions and vibrant festivals that form the tapestry of Hong Kong's cultural heritage.

Whether you're planning a short stopover or an extended stay, our travel guide will provide you with invaluable information on transportation, accommodations, local customs, and the best time to visit. We will also offer insights into the unique blend of

Chinese and Western influences that shape Hong Kong's architecture, arts, and entertainment scene.

So, get ready to embark on an unforgettable journey through the dynamic city of Hong Kong. Let us be your guide as you uncover the hidden treasures and vibrant spirit that make this metropolis a must-visit destination for travelers from around the globe.

# CHAPTER ONE

## History Culture and Geography of Hong Kong

Hong Kong is a vibrant and dynamic city that boasts a rich history, diverse culture, and unique geography.

**History:**

The history of Hong Kong dates back thousands of years. The region was originally inhabited by indigenous people, who were later joined by Chinese immigrants. In the 19th century, Hong Kong became a British colony after the First Opium War. Under British rule, the city prospered as a major trading port and developed into an important financial center in Asia.

In 1997, Hong Kong was returned to China under the "one country, two systems" principle, which granted it a high degree of autonomy and allowed the city to maintain its capitalist economic system and legal framework. Today, Hong Kong is a Special Administrative Region of China.

## Culture:

Hong Kong's culture is a unique blend of Eastern and Western influences. Its colonial history has left a lasting impact on the city's cultural fabric. Traditional Chinese customs and festivals are widely celebrated, including Chinese New Year, the Mid-Autumn Festival, and the Dragon Boat Festival. The city is also home to numerous temples, such as Wong Tai Sin Temple and Man Mo Temple, where locals and visitors pay their respects.

Hong Kong's cosmopolitan nature is reflected in its thriving arts and entertainment scene. The city hosts international film festivals, art exhibitions, and theater performances. Additionally, Hong Kong has its film industry, known as

"Cantonese cinema," which has produced influential directors and actors.

The cuisine is an integral part of Hong Kong's culture. It offers a wide array of culinary delights, ranging from traditional Cantonese dim sum to international cuisine. Hong Kong is known for its street food culture, with bustling night markets and food stalls offering a variety of flavors and dishes.

## Geography:

Situated on the southeastern coast of China, Hong Kong is known for its stunning geography. The region comprises Hong Kong Island, the Kowloon Peninsula, the New Territories, and over 200 outlying islands. The city is surrounded by the South China Sea, giving it a picturesque waterfront.

Hong Kong's topography is characterized by its iconic skyline, mountainous terrain, and beautiful hiking trails. Victoria Peak, the highest point on Hong Kong Island, offers panoramic views of the city's skyline. The city's abundance of green spaces, such as Hong Kong Park and Kowloon Park, provide a respite from the urban hustle and bustle.

The city's harbor, Victoria Harbour, is renowned for its natural beauty and serves as a major transportation hub. It separates Hong Kong Island from the Kowloon Peninsula and provides a stunning backdrop to the city's skyline, especially during the Symphony of Lights, a nightly multimedia light and sound show.

# CHAPTER TWO

## Planning Your Trip

Planning a trip to Hong Kong can be an exciting and enriching experience. Known for its vibrant culture, stunning skyline, delicious cuisine, and unique blend of Eastern and Western influences, Hong Kong offers a wide range of attractions and activities to explore.

To make the most of your trip, here are some steps to help you plan your journey:

- Determine the Duration of Your Trip: Decide how long you want to stay in Hong Kong. Consider your budget, available vacation time, and the activities you wish to engage in. A typical visit can range from a few days to a week, but it ultimately depends on your preferences.

- Research and Choose the Best Time to Visit: Hong Kong has a subtropical climate, so it's important to consider the weather when planning your trip. The best time to visit is during the cooler months from October to December or from March to April when the weather is pleasant. However, Hong Kong is a year-round destination, so be prepared for warmer and more humid conditions during the summer months.

- Create an Itinerary: Research the attractions and activities that interest you and create a rough itinerary. Hong Kong offers a variety of experiences such as exploring the bustling streets, visiting historic sites, enjoying the vibrant nightlife, shopping, hiking, and experiencing the local cuisine. Make a list of the must-see places and prioritize them based on your interests and time available.

- Book Your Flights: Look for flights to Hong Kong and compare prices from different airlines. Consider factors such as layovers, travel time, and cost. Book your flights well in advance to secure the best deals. Hong Kong International Airport (HKG) is one of the busiest airports in Asia and offers excellent connectivity to various parts of the world.

- Find Accommodation: Hong Kong has a wide range of accommodation options to suit different budgets and preferences. Popular areas to stay include Central, Tsim Sha Tsui, Causeway Bay, and Mong Kok. Consider factors such as proximity to attractions, accessibility to public transportation, and the type of experience you want (luxury hotel, budget hostel, or serviced apartment). Book your accommodation in advance to secure the best rates.

- Understand Visa Requirements: Check the visa requirements for your nationality. Most nationalities enjoy visa-free access to Hong Kong for a limited period, typically ranging from 7 to 180 days. Ensure that your passport is valid for at least six months beyond your intended visit period.

- Learn Basic Local Etiquette and Customs: Familiarize yourself with Hong Kong's culture and customs to show respect and avoid any unintended offense. Learn a few basic Cantonese phrases such as greetings and simple expressions to enhance your interactions with the locals.

- Plan Your Transportation: Hong Kong has an efficient and extensive public transportation system, including the MTR (Mass Transit Railway), buses, trams, ferries, and taxis. Purchase an Octopus Card upon arrival, which can be used for multiple modes of transport and makes getting around the city more convenient.

- Budget and Money Matters: Determine your budget for the trip and allocate funds for accommodation, meals, transportation, attractions, shopping, and miscellaneous expenses. It's advisable to carry a mix of cash and credit cards. ATMs are available throughout the city, also, the use of credit cards are accepted in most establishments.

- Pack Accordingly: Check the weather forecast for your travel dates and pack suitable clothing. Hong Kong can be humid, so lightweight and breathable fabrics are recommended. Don't forget essentials such as comfortable walking shoes, sunscreen, an umbrella, and an adapter for your electronic devices.

- Purchase Travel Insurance: It's always wise to have travel insurance that covers medical emergencies, trip cancellation, and loss of belongings. Ensure the policy provides adequate coverage for your needs.

- Check Travel Advisories: Before your departure, check for any travel advisories or updates regarding Hong Kong. Keep track of any safety or health concerns that may affect your trip.

## CHAPTER THREE

## Major cities in Hong Kong and Transportation options

Hong Kong, a bustling metropolis known for its vibrant culture and thriving economy, offers a variety of transportation options to cater to the needs of both residents and visitors. Whether you're traveling to Hong Kong for business or leisure, you'll find an extensive network of airports, taxis, car rentals, and other means of transportation to explore the city and beyond.

**Airports:**

Hong Kong is served by Hong Kong International Airport (HKIA), one of the busiest airports in the world. Located on the island of Chek Lap Kok, HKIA offers excellent connectivity to various destinations worldwide. It features state-of-the-art facilities, including multiple passenger terminals, a wide range of dining and shopping options, and convenient transportation links to the city center.

## Taxis:
Taxis are a popular mode of transportation in Hong Kong, known for their efficiency and convenience. The city has three types of taxis: red, green, and blue. Red taxis operate throughout most of Hong Kong, including the urban areas of Kowloon and Hong Kong Island. Green taxis are restricted to the New Territories, while blue taxis exclusively serve Lantau Island, including the airport. Taxis in Hong Kong are metered, and fares are reasonable. However, keep in mind that traffic congestion during peak hours may affect travel times.

## Mass Transit Railway (MTR):
The Mass Transit Railway (MTR) is Hong Kong's efficient and extensive subway system. It covers major areas of Hong Kong, including the urban core, New Territories, and parts of Lantau Island. The MTR offers

a convenient way to travel quickly and comfortably between different districts. It features a comprehensive fare structure, allowing passengers to pay based on the distance traveled. The MTR network also connects to the airport, making it an accessible option for travelers.

## Buses:
Hong Kong has a comprehensive bus network that serves various parts of the city, including the urban areas and New Territories. The buses are operated by different companies, each with its routes and schedules. Bus fares are generally affordable, and the network covers both popular tourist areas and residential neighborhoods. However, keep in mind that buses can be affected by traffic congestion during peak hours.

## Trams:
One of the iconic transportation options in Hong Kong is the double-decker tram, also

known as "ding-dings" due to the sound of their bells. Trams primarily operate on Hong Kong Island, providing an affordable and scenic way to explore areas such as Central, Causeway Bay, and Wan Chai. Tram fares are inexpensive, and passengers can pay with Octopus cards or cash.

**Car Rentals:**
If you prefer the freedom and flexibility of driving, car rental services are available in Hong Kong. Several international and local car rental companies offer a range of vehicles to suit different needs. However, it's important to note that driving in Hong Kong can be challenging due to heavy traffic, limited parking spaces, and the city's complex road network. Additionally, Hong Kong has an excellent public transportation system, so renting a car may not be necessary for most visitors.

**Ferries:**

As an archipelago, Hong Kong has an extensive ferry network that connects the main islands and outlying areas. Ferries are commonly used for traveling to destinations like Lantau Island, Cheung Chau, Lamma Island, and Discovery Bay. These scenic boat rides offer a different perspective of Hong Kong's skyline and harbor.

# CHAPTER FOUR

## Accommodations (Hotels, Resorts, and Camping Sites)

**Top Hotels in Hong Kong:**

- The Peninsula Hong Kong: This iconic hotel offers luxurious accommodations with stunning harbor views, impeccable service, and world-class amenities.
- The Ritz-Carlton Hong Kong: Located in the International Commerce Centre, this hotel boasts panoramic views of the city and offers elegant rooms, Michelin-starred dining, and a rooftop pool.
- Mandarin Oriental, Hong Kong: Situated in the heart of the city, this hotel is renowned for its legendary service, stylish rooms, and exceptional dining options.
- Four Seasons Hotel Hong Kong: With its prime location on Victoria

Harbour, this hotel offers spacious rooms, a rooftop pool, and award-winning restaurants.

- Island Shangri-La Hong Kong: This luxury hotel features elegantly appointed rooms, breathtaking views of the city, and an array of dining options.
- The Upper House: Offering a tranquil retreat amidst the bustling city, this boutique hotel provides spacious rooms, personalized service, and a stylish rooftop restaurant.
- InterContinental Hong Kong: Located on the Kowloon waterfront, this hotel offers luxurious rooms, superb dining options, and breathtaking views of Victoria Harbour.
- The Landmark Mandarin Oriental: Known for its contemporary design and cutting-edge amenities, this hotel offers sleek rooms, a spa, and a Michelin-starred restaurant.

- The Langham Hong Kong: Combining classic elegance with modern comfort, this hotel offers stylish rooms, a rooftop pool, and a range of dining options.
- WHong Kong: Situated in West Kowloon, this trendy hotel features stylish rooms, a rooftop pool with panoramic views, and vibrant nightlife options.

## Top Resorts in Hong Kong:
- Auberge Discovery Bay Hong Kong: This beachfront resort offers a relaxed getaway on Lantau Island, with spacious rooms, a beach club, and a range of recreational activities.
- Hong Kong Disneyland Hotel: Perfect for families, this resort is located near Hong Kong Disneyland and offers themed rooms, a pool, and easy access to the park.
- Tai O Heritage Hotel: Set in a charming fishing village, this boutique

hotel provides a unique cultural experience with well-appointed rooms and picturesque surroundings.

- Noah's Ark Resort: Ideal for families and nature lovers, this resort on Ma Wan Island offers themed rooms, a private beach, and a variety of outdoor activities.
- Hong Kong Gold Coast Hotel: Nestled in a scenic waterfront location, this resort features spacious rooms, a lagoon-style pool, and a range of recreational facilities.
- Silvermine Beach Resort: Located on Lantau Island, this beachfront resort offers comfortable rooms, a swimming pool, and easy access to hiking trails and water sports.
- Royal View Hotel: Situated in Tsuen Wan, this resort offers panoramic views of the city and the harbor, spacious rooms, and a range of dining options.

- Hong Kong Ocean Park Marriott Hotel: Connected to Ocean Park, this resort provides convenient access to the theme park, along with modern rooms, a pool, and dining options.
- Bay Bridge Hong Kong by Hotel G: Located in Tsuen Wan, this resort offers spacious serviced apartments with stunning harbor views, a rooftop pool, and a fitness center.
- L'hotel Nina et Convention Centre: Featuring contemporary rooms and extensive facilities, this resort in Tsuen Wan offers stunning views, a pool, and a range of dining options.

**Top Camping Sites in Hong Kong:**
- Sai Yuen Farm, Cheung Chau: This unique camping site offers a variety of accommodation options, including luxury tents, tree houses, and beachside camping.
- Tai Long Wan, Sai Kung: Known for its picturesque beaches and hiking

trails, this area offers camping options with beautiful coastal views.

- Pui O Campsite, Lantau Island: Situated near Pui O Beach, this campsite provides facilities such as barbecue pits, toilets, and showers, and offers a peaceful camping experience.
- High Island Reservoir East Dam Campsite, Sai Kung: Located near the stunning High Island Reservoir, this campsite offers breathtaking views and is a popular spot for stargazing.
- Tai Tam Tuk Reservoir Campsite, Hong Kong Island: Set amidst the lush greenery of Tai Tam Country Park, this campsite offers tranquil surroundings and facilities for camping enthusiasts.
- Ma On Shan Barbecue Site, Ma On Shan: While primarily a barbecue site, this location also allows camping and provides a serene atmosphere amid nature.

- Lantau Island Youth Camp, Lantau Island: This campsite offers basic facilities and affordable accommodation options, allowing visitors to explore the natural beauty of Lantau Island.
- Tung Ping Chau, Northeast New Territories: This remote island is a designated UNESCO Global Geopark and offers camping opportunities surrounded by unique rock formations and scenic landscapes.
- Yuen Tsuen Ancient Trail Campsite, Tsuen Wan: Located along the historic Yuen Tsuen Ancient Trail, this campsite provides a rustic camping experience with beautiful natural surroundings.
- Lung Mun Oasis Campsite, Tuen Mun: Set in Tuen Mun, this campsite offers a peaceful retreat with camping facilities and is an excellent option for outdoor enthusiasts.

# CHAPTER FIVE

## Ancient Monuments, Museums, and Shopping Malls alls in Hong Kong

**Ancient Monuments in Hong Kong:**

- Wong Tai Sin Temple: A popular Taoist temple known for its beautiful architecture and colorful decorations.
- Man Mo Temple: A historic temple dedicated to the gods of literature (Man) and war (Mo), featuring large hanging incense coils.
- Po Lin Monastery: Home to the iconic Tian Tan Buddha statue, this monastery offers a serene and picturesque environment.
- Sik Sik Yuen Wong Shek Temple: A tranquil Buddhist temple with traditional Chinese architectural elements.
- Tsing Ma Bridge: Although not ancient in the traditional sense, this

suspension bridge is an engineering marvel and a prominent landmark.

- Tung Chung Fort: A well-preserved Qing dynasty fortress that once guarded the entrance to Tung Chung Bay.
- Kowloon Walled City Park: Originally a military stronghold, this park now preserves the history of the former walled city through exhibits and artifacts.
- Yuen Long Old Market: A traditional market that has been operating for over a century, showcasing the local culture and traditional shops.
- Kat Hing Wai Walled Village: An ancient walled village with a rich history and well-preserved architecture.
- Tai Fu Tai Mansion: A stately residence built in the 19th century, showcasing the opulence and craftsmanship of the era.

**Museums in Hong Kong:**

- Hong Kong Museum of History: Offers a comprehensive overview of Hong Kong's history and culture through engaging exhibits.
- Hong Kong Heritage Museum: Showcases the art, history, and culture of Hong Kong, with a focus on local traditions and customs.
- Hong Kong Science Museum: Features interactive exhibits on science, technology, and natural history, appealing to visitors of all ages.
- Flagstaff House Museum of Tea Ware: Housed in a colonial-era building, this museum explores the art and culture of tea drinking in China.
- Hong Kong Maritime Museum: Traces the maritime history of Hong Kong and its importance as a trading port.
- Dr. Sun Yat-sen Museum: Commemorates the life and achievements of Dr. Sun Yat-sen,

known as the founding father of modern China.

- Lei Cheng Uk Han Tomb Museum: Displays a well-preserved ancient tomb and artifacts from the Han dynasty.
- Hong Kong Museum of Art: Showcases a wide range of Chinese and international art, including paintings, calligraphy, and ceramics.
- Hong Kong Railway Museum: Offers insights into the history of Hong Kong's railways and showcases vintage locomotives.
- Hong Kong Space Museum: Features astronomy and space science exhibits, including a planetarium and an Omnimax theater.

## Shopping Destinations in Hong Kong:
- Causeway Bay: Known for its luxury shopping malls, trendy boutiques, and bustling street markets.

- Tsim Sha Tsui: Offers a wide range of shopping options, including high-end brands, electronics, and local street markets.
- Mong Kok: Famous for its bustling street markets, night markets, and diverse range of shops selling fashion, electronics, and more.
- Central: Home to upscale designer stores, luxury shopping malls, and international fashion brands.
- Times Square: A large shopping mall in Causeway Bay with a mix of luxury and high-street brands.
- Harbor City: Located in Tsim Sha Tsui, it is one of the largest shopping malls in Hong Kong, offering a vast selection of fashion, beauty, and lifestyle stores.
- Pacific Place: A premium shopping mall in Admiralty, known for its luxury brands and upscale dining options.

- Temple Street Night Market: Famous for its lively atmosphere and wide range of affordable clothing, accessories, and street food.
- Stanley Market: Located in the charming Stanley Village, this market is known for its souvenirs, clothing, and home decor items.
- Ladies' Market: Situated in Mong Kok, it offers a variety of affordable fashion items, accessories, and souvenirs, primarily targeting female shoppers.

# CHAPTER SIX

## Local Cuisines, Drinks, and Street Food in Hong Kong

### Local Cuisines in Hong Kong:

- Dim Sum: These bite-sized portions of steamed or fried dumplings, buns, and rolls are a staple of Cantonese cuisine. Popular dim sum dishes include siu mai, har gow, and char siu bao.

- Roast Goose: Hong Kong-style roast goose is a must-try dish. The goose is marinated in a flavorful blend of spices and herbs, then roasted until the skin becomes crispy and the meat tender and succulent.

- Wonton Noodles: Wontons are small dumplings filled with seasoned minced meat, usually served in a clear broth with thin egg noodles. The dish is often garnished with green onions and a sprinkle of sesame oil.

- Clay Pot Rice: This dish is prepared by cooking rice, marinated meats, and vegetables in a clay pot. The result is a deliciously fragrant and flavorful one-pot meal.

- Pineapple Bun with Butter: A popular Hong Kong-style pastry, the pineapple bun is a sweet bun with a crunchy, sugary crust resembling a pineapple. It is often served with a thick slice of cold butter in the center.

- Egg Tart: Influenced by Portuguese cuisine, the Hong Kong-style egg tart features a flaky crust filled with a smooth and creamy egg custard. It is best enjoyed fresh from the oven.

- Beef Brisket Noodles: Slow-cooked beef brisket served with chewy noodles in a flavorful broth is a comforting and hearty dish that is popular among locals.

- Curry Fish Balls: Fish balls, made from minced fish paste, are cooked in a fragrant curry sauce. They are typically served on skewers and make for a popular street snack.

- Stinky Tofu: While the smell might be off-putting to some, stinky tofu is a beloved street food in Hong Kong. The fermented tofu is deep-fried until crispy on the outside and soft on the inside.

- Hong Kong-style Milk Tea: A strong and creamy blend of black tea and evaporated milk, Hong Kong-style milk tea is a beloved beverage that can be enjoyed hot or iced. It is a popular accompaniment to local breakfasts.

## Local Drinks in Hong Kong:

- Yuanyang: A popular local beverage, yuan yang is a blend of coffee and Hong Kong-style milk tea. It combines the best of both worlds, offering a unique flavor that is both rich and creamy.

- Lemon Iced Tea: Refreshing and tangy, lemon iced tea is a popular choice during hot summer months. It is a perfect thirst quencher to combat the heat.

- Herbal Tea: Hong Kong is known for its wide variety of herbal teas, which are believed to have medicinal properties. These teas are made from a combination of herbs, flowers, and roots and are often served hot.

- Red Bean Ice: A popular dessert drink, red bean ice is a sweet and creamy beverage made from blended red beans, crushed ice, and sweetened condensed milk.

- Fresh Sugarcane Juice: Sugarcane juice is extracted by pressing sugarcane stalks and is a refreshing and natural beverage choice in Hong Kong.

- Mango Sago: Made with fresh mangoes, sago pearls, and coconut milk, this tropical drink is sweet, creamy, and incredibly satisfying.

- Hong Kong-style Iced Coffee: Known for its strong and bold flavor, Hong Kong-style iced coffee is made by pouring hot coffee directly over a glass filled with ice, resulting in a refreshing and energizing beverage.

- Winter Melon Tea: This cooling and soothing drink is made from winter melon, a type of gourd with a naturally sweet taste. It is often served chilled and is a popular choice to quench thirst in the summer.

- Grass Jelly Drink: Grass jelly, a jelly-like dessert made from the leaves of a Chinese herb, is often served in sweet syrup or mixed with other ingredients to create a refreshing and cooling drink.

- Chrysanthemum                Tea: Chrysanthemum tea is a popular herbal infusion made from dried chrysanthemum flowers. It has a delicate floral aroma and is often consumed hot or cold.

## Street Food in Hong Kong:
- Curry Fish Balls: These bite-sized fish balls are cooked in a spicy curry sauce and skewered for easy eating. They are a quintessential street food in Hong Kong.

- Siu Mai: These steamed dumplings are filled with a mixture of ground pork, shrimp, and other ingredients, and are a popular street snack.

- Egg Waffles (Gai Dan Jai): This iconic Hong Kong street food is made by cooking a sweet batter on a special griddle, resulting in a bubbly and crispy waffle with a soft interior.

- Grilled Squid Skewers: Squid is marinated, grilled, and served on a skewer with a spicy or savory sauce. It is a flavorful and satisfying street food option.

- Curry Fish Balls: Fish balls are cooked in a savory and spicy curry sauce, resulting in a delicious and addictive street food snack.

- Egg Tarts: Freshly baked egg tarts are a popular street food item in Hong Kong. The flaky crust and creamy custard filling make for a delightful treat.

- Bubble Waffles: Also known as "egg puffs," bubble waffles are made by pouring a sweet batter into a special griddle, creating a lattice-like pattern. The result is a crispy and chewy waffle that can be enjoyed plain or with various toppings.

- Cheung Fun: These steamed rice noodle rolls are typically filled with ingredients like shrimp, beef, or char siu (barbecued pork) and drizzled with a sweet soy sauce.

- Stuffed Tofu Puffs: Tofu puffs are stuffed with a mixture of fish paste or minced pork, then deep-fried to perfection. They are often served with a sweet and savory sauce.

- Pineapple Skewers: Fresh pineapple chunks are skewered and grilled to enhance their natural sweetness. They make for a delicious and healthy street snack.

# CHAPTER SEVEN

## Vaccines and Emergency Management

As a popular destination for tourists, Hong Kong places a strong emphasis on ensuring the health and safety of its visitors. Vaccinations and emergency management play crucial roles in safeguarding the well-being of tourists and residents alike. Here's an overview of the measures taken in Hong Kong concerning vaccinations and emergency management for tourists.

## Vaccinations in Hong Kong:

Hong Kong has a robust vaccination program aimed at protecting its population against various diseases. Tourists visiting Hong Kong are strongly encouraged to stay up to date with their routine vaccinations and consider additional vaccinations based on their travel plans and individual health conditions. The most common vaccines recommended for travelers to Hong Kong include:

- Routine vaccines: These include vaccinations such as measles-mumps-rubella (MMR), diphtheria-tetanus-pertussis, varicella (chickenpox), and influenza.
- Hepatitis A and B: Hepatitis A is recommended for all travelers, while Hepatitis B is recommended for those who may have intimate contact with locals or engage in activities that may expose them to blood or other body fluids.
- Typhoid: Recommended for travelers who may consume food or water in areas with poor sanitation.
- Japanese encephalitis: Recommended for those planning to visit rural areas or engage in extensive outdoor activities.

Tourists should consult their healthcare providers or travel clinics well in advance of their trip to receive personalized advice on vaccinations.

## COVID-19 Considerations:

In light of the ongoing COVID-19 pandemic, Hong Kong has implemented stringent measures to mitigate the spread of the virus. Tourists should stay informed about the latest travel restrictions, quarantine requirements, and entry protocols before planning their trip. Hong Kong has also initiated its vaccination program, offering COVID-19 vaccines to residents and eligible visitors. Tourists should check if they meet the criteria for vaccination and consider getting vaccinated before traveling to Hong Kong.

## Emergency Management:

Hong Kong has a well-established emergency management system to ensure the safety of residents and visitors in case of unforeseen events. The Hong Kong Special Administrative Region Government closely monitors the situation and provides regular updates through various channels, including the Hong Kong Observatory, the Department of Health, and the Immigration Department. These agencies work together to address emergencies promptly and efficiently.

In the event of an emergency, tourists should follow the instructions and guidelines issued by the local authorities. It is advisable to register with your embassy or consulate and keep their contact details handy. Tourists should also maintain travel insurance that covers medical emergencies and evacuation if necessary.

**Tourism-related Information:**
The Hong Kong Tourism Board (HKTB) serves as a valuable treasure for tourists, providing them with up-to-date information on safety, health advisories, and emergency management. The HKTB website offers comprehensive guides and travel tips to help

tourists make informed decisions and stay safe during their visit to Hong Kong.

# CHAPTER EIGHT

## Basic Greetings in Hong Kong

In Hong Kong, greetings can vary depending on the context and the relationship between individuals. Here are a few common ways to greet people in Hong Kong:

- Ni hao (你好): This is a simple and widely used greeting that means "hello" in Mandarin Chinese. It can be used in formal and informal situations.

- Lei ho (你好): This is the Cantonese equivalent of "hello." Cantonese is the most commonly spoken language in Hong Kong, so this greeting is widely understood and used.

- Haak hei (學嘢): This is a casual way to say "What's up" or "How's it going" in Cantonese. It's commonly used among friends and peers.

- Gam1 sa1 jou6 (感謝你): This is the Cantonese phrase for "thank you." It's always polite to express gratitude when someone helps you or provides a service.

- Jo sun (早晨): This means "good morning" in Cantonese. It's often used in the early hours of the day as a greeting to wish someone a good morning.

Remember that Hong Kong is a multicultural city, and English is widely spoken, especially in more formal or professional settings. So, using "hello" or "hi" in English is also generally accepted and understood. If you're unsure, it's always best to start with a polite and friendly greeting and follow the lead of the person you're speaking to.

## CONCLUSION

In conclusion, Hong Kong is a vibrant and dynamic city that offers a plethora of attractions, cultural experiences, and culinary delights. Whether you are a history buff, a nature enthusiast, a shopaholic, or a food lover, this city has something to offer everyone. From the iconic Victoria Peak, where you can soak in breathtaking views of the skyline, to the bustling markets of Mong Kok and the tranquil beaches of Sai Kung, Hong Kong's diverse range of activities ensures that there is never a dull moment.

Exploring the city's rich history and culture is a must, with attractions such as the historic Man Mo Temple and the awe-inspiring Wong Tai Sin Temple. For those seeking entertainment, Hong Kong Disneyland and Ocean Park provide fun-filled experiences for visitors of all ages. Additionally, the city's world-class shopping scene, from luxury brand boutiques to bustling street markets like the Ladies Market, will leave even the most avid shoppers satisfied.

Hong Kong's culinary scene is legendary, offering a melting pot of flavors from both traditional Cantonese cuisine and international fare. Dim sum, roasted meats, and seafood delicacies are just a few highlights of the local food scene, and exploring the city's street food stalls is an adventure in itself.

Printed in Great Britain
by Amazon

25883834R00030